I Got This!

Eve Brownstone

To
Francine,
You Got
This!
♡ EB

For everyone who has taught me about Love

Table of Contents

A Place to Begin

"What you are seeking is seeking you."
- Rumi

Thinking about Love

This year I thought about love.

I wrote a book of love poems.

Thinking and feeling love are two different animals.

One is full of tulips and chocolates the other has teeth and Dragon breath.

For god sakes I was married.

Not sure I know what Love is….

Love can be Scary

This year I received over 200 happy birthday wishes on Facebook.

The next day I sobbed.

My heart was overwhelmed with so much love.

What's wrong with me?

Why does love freak me out?

This is Where it Started

I make people prove themselves to me with money, food, time, or feelings. You must love me exactly the way I want. In turn, I feel like I have to be a certain way to be loved. It has been hard for me to see others as separate from me. This could be due to being an identical twin. It has taken me longer to grow up. I am growing and learning to be Eve.

I decided this year to stop pushing myself into my constant dance of doing and just give myself time to: sit with me, learn about me, and maybe even learn to trust me. Wow, what a concept! I can trust and even like me. But, it takes daily commitment to show up for me and not everybody else.

Maybe if I give myself a break from being a certain way I can give others a break.

Taking care of everybody else even if they didn't want or need my help just comes naturally to me. It often goes like this:

EVE: Let me help you!

THEM: NO!

EVE: Let me help you!

THEM: NO! I don't need anything from you. I don't love you. I don't care about you. You are unlovable! (What I hear.)

The worst! It feels like bumper cars. I never hear:

I am not interested. I am ok. I don't need your help, but I would like your company.

Someone really seeing me scares the shit out of me. It's also what I long for the most. My idea of love pushes back and teaches me to stop and listen to my own heart. I need to just stop

running from my feelings,

running from myself,

running from my own life

This book is my personal journey, but it pulls on universal themes of connection, identity, love, freedom, loneliness, and choice. As you read it just ask yourself:

What does love feel like for me? How can I love myself more?

A Little Self-Love

This week I got back to the beach.

I got back to the sunrise.

It's a time of day between 5am-8am
when I feel most connected with myself and my higher power.

I sit in the quiet of the waves and the seagulls and hear myself breathe.

For me a perfect day starts and ends at the beach in stillness or play.

More of what I love:

Hanging out with family and friends

Laughing

Hearing people's stories

Being myself

Writing in a coffee shop

Painting on canvas

Dancing with silly partners

Not taking myself too seriously and being with people who do the same

Questions about Love

When it is all said and done:

Is it enough to make each other laugh and fold the laundry in your underwear?

Do you have to feel over-powered with feelings for the other person
or can it just be gentle comfort and sweet quiet,
where neither of you have to talk?

Getting There...

"In between good and evil there is a garden. I'll meet you there."
-Rumi

Daddy's Girl

As a little girl I liked to hold my Daddy's hand and ride on his shoulders. I felt taller and loved. He was a big bad tickle monster and told the spookiest stories

like the Monkey Claw!

He chased a real bad guy down an alley with an hatchet after he tried to hurt Laura and I.

My Hero!

When I had the good fortune to be cast in The Winter's Tale at Court Theater, Dad drove me to rehearsals. It was a little bit of our time together. I was a bit of a show off…still am…and I liked to show off for my Dad.

I have fond members in Akron of being woken up every morning by Dad

"It's time to rise and shine," he'd say.

I was a teenager. I didn't really want to wake up. Looking back on it though, I do appreciate that early morning wake up and the car rides to school.

My relationship with Dad hasn't always been sunshine. He and I got into some hellish yelling matches when I was in high school.

I blamed him for our parents divorce.

It always takes two to tango.

Love you Dad.

All I See Is You / Where Am I?

All I see is you.

Your eyes. Your voice.

You are asking me a question.

I can't hear you.

How can I hear you, if all I see is you?

I don't see my eyes or hear my voice.

I touch my arm but in my eyes your hand
Is touching your arm.

Where is my hand? Where is my arm?

Is our breath the same as my breath?

Can you keep air in my lungs?

If I scream, do I use my own mouth?

I want to scream with my own mouth!

I want to see my own mouth.

Out of Body

As a kid I was a running,

jumping,

roller-skating

kind of kid.

I was active and in my body.

At the age of nine, I was doing gymnastics and learning to flip-flop, but also to leave my body.

During a long hot car ride, I was being my usual annoying self or just being a kid. My father was driving and mom was next to me in the back seat of our station wagon. I don't know what I said or did, but my father grabbed my leg and started hitting it and my mother next to me started slapping my upper body....

I know I fucking just fucking left my body. It seemed like it went on forever. Probably lasted a few seconds, but I learned that I wasn't safe.

Next thing I know mom is crying in a motel room. I sit down next to her on the bed and say, "It's ok. I am ok, mom." I learned in those moments that I wasn't safe and that it was my job to comfort.

Co-dependency was born!

It wasn't ok! I wasn't ok.

It was mom and dad's job to keep me safe and comfort me.

I was just nine.

Dancing Queen

From the Tap Dance Gym Show
"Fire Boom Boom Boom"
I learned I had some moves.

I knew all the words and dances to Grease.
My twin and baby-sister and I would act Grease out everyday,
seemed like it anyway for weeks,
months
not years
ok, maybe years.
Grease and Saturday Night Fever
Travolta
What a hottie!

I so wanted to be seen.
I wanted to be seen for myself,
not just as one of the twins.

I wanted people to like me.
Performing was my way of getting attention.

Chicago Children's Choir, Gymnastics, Summer Stock Theater
At ten I remember asking everyone at the JCC summer camp
"Are you coming to my play?"
People had to say yes.
Some did and some didn't.
I took it personally when another ten year old had no interest in
Shakespeare.

Bastards….

Funny thing though:
Before I would perform I felt petrified.

Throwing up before a concert— it was at Ravinia with the Joffrey Ballet.
Come on people…
I performed and years later, the Artistic Director of The Joffrey Ballet
remembered me because I was the kid who threw up.

——

Mom was there.
Mom was there for my gymnastics meets.
Mom was there when I was so nervous before competing
and afterwards when I needed to take a day off of school to recover.

I was a brave girl,
but I also got scared

Still scared of the dark
Scared of riding a bike
Scared of falling in love
Yes, really.

But I did things not everyone could do:
I performed for five hundred sets of twins at the Twin Day Festival
and spoke in front of millions as a Twin expert.
Chaired MidSommarfest and was President of a nonprofit arts board

I have had a life
my own way.
Maybe I am still figuring out the real me?
I seem to base my sense of self on other people's perceptions of me.
It's not really working for me anymore.

Shut Up and Go to Your Room

"Shut up and go to your room!!"
I would hear frequently.
I would go to my room and slam the door.
I got really good at that.

I was a fearless girl until the age of seven.
I liked to say stuff,
Speak up,
make up songs.
I learned how to flip,
how to be silly,
play tag
and red light green light with
Connie, Karen, Laura, Stacey, and Kanita.
I was a happy little one.

At the age of seven, my father started pulling away
and my mother pushed me away.

I remember trying to learn to ride a bike.
Today, I break out in sweats
whenever I get on a bike.
I am getting there.
I know when
I do stay on and ride a bike,
I will grow up a little more.
I'll let go of the yelling and the shame.

My parents did the best they could.
It wasn't fucking good enough!
I felt squashed and scared.

What about that brave little girl
that just wanted love,
and to be heard,
and seen?

———

Fierce Girl

If a look could tell a thousand stories,
her look would tell a million.

She doesn't pretend.
She doesn't apologize.
She has walked through the fires and is alive,
but just barely. She is alive.
Fuck you!

She knows herself more
She knows she will do anything to survive.
She'll claw her way onto a plane,
fights the monsters who tried to break her in two.

She speaks her mind.
She speak for the quieted and the scared
in herself and others.

Don't fuck with her.
She is beautiful. She will bite.
She is a terror to be reckoned with.

Does she look kind to you?
Hell, No!!!!

Precious Girl

What do you need precious girl?

Attention. Lots and lots of it,
someone's undivided attention,
my papa's attention,
my mama's attention

I am such a good girl.
See how good I am trying to be?
Perfect and smiling,
so sweet,
such an angel.
Fuck you
is more like it.

I want to know the real you.
Not just your pretty sweet face,
but your wild and feisty open heart.

I see you.
Maybe I don't want to be seen?
You just said you wanted lots of attention.
Maybe I was lying?
Maybe I was just telling you
what you wanted to hear?

Why is that? Why can't you be real with me?

I am an angry and bitchy fat girl
who doesn't know what she wants.
You won't like her – me.
You won't want to talk with me
or touch me if I get too close.
I might even kill with my love.
People who get too close to me
die.
Afraid yet?

No. I am not afraid of death or you.

What do you want precious girl?

Not sure what I really want.
Never thought I could get what I wanted,
so I stopped asking,
stopped wondering and wanting,
stopped living.

Are you happy now?
That you feel like you are dead inside?

No.

I am happy you are being honest with me
for the first time in your life.

What do you really want?

Warrior of the Dark Forest

The Warrior of the Dark Forest cuts to the joint and rips the rest with her bare hands. Blood is everywhere, but mainly on her. She takes limbs, hearts and skin. The cuts are deep and shake her. She is tired, but she battles through the night, not knowing any different.

Take her sword.
Take her hand.
Take her out of the Dark to the Beach.
Hide her blade.
Give her your heart,
in something as gentle as a smile.
Don't tell her you love her.
She will cut your head from your neck.
She is good at that.

Fuck off,
Stay away.

I can kill all of you with my vicious Love.

Humans are Complicated

Humans are complicated.

I am a good person,
but I am no angel.
If I like you I will call you a "Bastard".
Or better yet "Mother Fucker".
It's all in the tone and context.

Cussing at you means I feel safe with you.
I might be pissed off in the moment.
Isn't it better to be called a Fucker than it is to have me quietly seething
passive- aggressively at you all day under clinched teeth?
I cuss and then let it go.
If you call me a "Fucker" back it might make us both laugh.
If you ask me how I am doing after you fuck with me and I say "I am fine,"

You are in fucking trouble.

There is something so freeing about saying:
"You Mother Fucking Cock Sucker."

I encourage my clients to cuss in session and in life.
Many of my clients are very nice people and don't give themselves
permission to tell someone to fuck off.

I encourage it.

As an Expressive Therapist,
I know cussing reduces:
Stress,
Depression,
Anxiety,
Insomnia…
It even boosts the immune system!

As a human being it feels very loving.

Give it a try.

Do I Repel You?

Do I repel you?
It's a legitimate question.
I open my mouth and people are leaving my life right and left.
I understand friends grow apart,
have disagreements,
get pissed off...

Fuck–Bottom line, Eve!
Not everyone is going to like you.
Get used to it my dear.
Put on your big-girl pants!

Please, how many people can I get to stop talking with me this month?
Last month I lost count.

Ok, the common denominator is you, so reflect:
Are you being real with people?
Real with yourself? Being kind?
Are you being passive aggressive?
Are you showing up for you or are you projecting your lovely anger into the world?
Do you even like these people who are leaving your life?

Some of them I love.

No I Didn't

Fuck you

Fuck you

Love you

Fuck you

Fuck you

Why the fuck are you walking away?

You told me to fuck off.

No I didn't…

Want to Fight?

You want to fight?
I want to hold your hand.

You want to put me in the dark and shut the door?
I just want to make us some tea.

You want to take away my stuff?
I don't want anything from you.

Go ahead. I know you want to punch me on the chin.
I don't want to punch you. I wanted to give you a hug.

I don't get this lovey dovey business.
It feels like as I get closer to you, you just get more scared.

I know fighting. I know people leaving without saying goodbye.
What is this handholding and hugging?

Maybe I should go?
Why do you want to go?
You don't seem to want anything I am offering. I go where I am wanted.

Stepping away.
Don't go.
Why?
I don't want you to go?
Why?
That's not a good enough reason for me to stay.

I love you and this is scaring the shit out of me. I don't know how to do this.
I don't know how to love.

You can start by loving yourself more, then we'll talk.

What Are You Afraid Of?

Feeling scared.
What are you afraid of?
Curling up in a ball.
What are you really fucking afraid of?
Facing my fucking shit.
Saying out loud outside of myself:
What the fuck happened to me?

I feel afraid like I'm naked and have no voice. I think I must have done something horrible to men in a past life.

What the fuck! Yes, there is Karma, but what about your feelings? This is not about beating yourself up or thinking you're a slut and a nothing. You learned to believe that about yourself. You can rewrite that story.

You were sobbing on the floor. A friend called you on your shit about how you always distract yourself from staring down the face of your own dark shadows. He isn't putting up with your BS and neither should you.

Oh, go fuck yourself!

Eve, I want to hear what you have to say.

Here goes a telling of some of what happened to me.

You feel so good. Look how pretty you are.
Oh, go fuck yourself?
Maybe I have given you HIV.
Oh, go fuck your crazy ass self.

Let's do it. You've done it with everybody.
No! No! No fucking NO!!!

 I can have you when I want you.
This is my pussy. I can beat it if I want.
I can hurt you if I want to.
Doesn't that turn you on?

Fuck you! Fuck you!!

You fucking hurt me.
You were the best rapist
I ever had.
Go fuck yourself.

You are someone
I have seen from time to time.
We are just dating.
You aren't my girlfriend.

I thought we were together.
I see you with someone else.

I have to be ok with it.
Don't make a scene.

We were sleeping together three days ago.
Three fucking days ago you told me you love me.

Fuck you. Fuck you.
You can't help yourself.

What is the common denominator here? Me.

Getting involved with men I can help.
I forget about what I want and get distracted.

From what?
From really being vulnerable.
Being myself.
Being not in control.
It scares the shit out of me.

You think you have to hurt like you've been hurt in the past?
You're speaking up for yourself and setting boundaries. This will protect
you.
Love is scary, but it won't destroy you (maybe your ego if you are lucky).
Love will inspire you and make you grow,
if you are with someone who is your equal.
You won't be inspired or grow if you are with someone
who has more of his own dark shadows to face and won't.
Keep looking at your dark shadows.

——

30

This is a doorway for you, Eve.
You are courageous.
This is for you to open and nobody else.
You got a chunk out and I am proud of you.

I love you.

What are you afraid of?

Not Five Anymore

STALKING is cute when you are five, but not when you are almost 50. I used to be the girl who would chase cute boys around the playground at recess. Later, I would get serious crushes, but never really act on it in high school. Deep down I didn't feel like I was lovable. And I always loved people who were just out of my reach.

I had an insecure attachment to my mother and father. I felt rejected by my mother as a little one and my father as a teenager. Both parents acknowledged what happened later and apologized, but a pattern was already set in motion. A life time of codependency and hurt was born. All I wanted was love and attention. I tried so hard to be good, to be noticed, to prove I was lovable. It really sucked.

I have a nasty habit of having an all-consuming crush on someone and then pursuing their friend. It happened in high school once, then again in my twenties after graduate school. I convinced myself that I loved a lovely man from South Africa, but when he didn't reciprocate I started dating his good friend. What was up with that? The other lovely man and I dated for a year. And I continued to have a crush on the first one. I even went to visit him after he moved. Something could have happened between us, but I stopped myself. I was really confused. I think I have been very confused about love all my life and about what I want or need. Bottom line: I have been looking outside of myself for love.

My ex-husband was into another woman at the time we met, and yet I still pursued him. I wanted to be with someone. He made me laugh. He liked to swim and take long walks on the beach. He seemed to know things. He seemed so in control. I gave up my power with him. There were moments when we loved. I am grateful for those moments and having the opportunity to start an arts nonprofit organization. I've been divorced for thirteen years now. In my forties, I loved a man. I knew he loved me back. I learned about unconditional love from him. Many times he pursued other women. I reached a point where I realized the relationship was hurtful and codependent for me and I pulled away from him.

I also get involved with people and projects that I feel are bigger than me. It brings a sense of meaning (again – outside of myself) like nonprofits, art galleries, and community organizations. I like to be of service and dig my teeth into something that matters. Usually the guys I've

32

hooked up with are visionaries. They are forces of nature to make new things happen. Maybe I am the visionary? I make stuff happen too.

In an effort to make something happen with a new guy, I acted out sort of stalkerish. I am not proud of my behavior. I felt all the familiar feelings. I believed myself to have fallen in love with a talented, real, and inspiring guy. I felt giddy and tingly when I would see him and be with him. It was a crush. The idea of him made me feel sparkly. For a week I couldn't stop smiling.

At the same time, I was running from heartache. I was running from my feelings. That is what I do, what I have done. Please don't run after love. Feel your feelings.

The brand new guy,
he told me I was
"awesome, rocked,
and that I was
beautiful."
I ate that stuff up.
I wrote many poems.
I felt inspired to
gush,
cry,
and dream.

But was it love?

Maybe. Sure there was chemistry on both sides…

He thought of me as slightly stalking him.
I don't blame him. I was. I don't like that part of me.

A few days after we messed around a little, I showed up at a meeting for an open mic that he frequented. It freaked him out. I told myself I did this because I wanted to be a part of writing/creative community. Over the next year I did actually grow to be an active and loyal part of this community. If I were honest with myself I'd admit that I showed up there because I was driven to see him again. I couldn't just let go and let things happen naturally. Co-dependency roared its ugly head again. One time he put out on social media that he was injured and I felt compelled to show up at his place with food.

"Stop Eve," I would tell myself.
But I did it anyway.

There was another guy who for years made me feel weak in the knees. Butterflies swirled in my stomach every time I saw him. He was refreshing for my soul too. I watched him grow into a man of heart and wisdom. We had some moments over those years, conversations that helped change my thinking and made me more expansive.

These two were buddies. It gets a little crazier right about now. I messed around with both of them. No sexual intercourse, but plenty of touching and sharing energy. At some point I thought that the first guy sent the second guy to me. In my mind, we had this unspoken understanding. I think that may have been just my delusional thinking. Not sure why. I did this. On some level it felt good. Somehow I convinced myself that they both cared for me. I liked the playful flirting and my body liked the touching. I could let go a little bit. I liked the attention. I had two beautiful men in my apartment – no, not at the same time! My fantasy had come true. I have been celibate for way too long. The shit really hit the fan (in my brain anyway) when I saw those two had a private meeting. I was convinced that they were talking about me. I proceeded to have a panic attack. Not a sign of good health.

Neither of these men are in my life much these days. One moved far away and the other moved on to greener pastures. I am grateful to them for teaching me more about Love and myself.

So, I am learning.
I continue to learn and love.
I am learning to love myself more
everyday and about that
I feel more hopeful.
Trying not to judge or beat myself up.
Just trying to understand this pattern and let it go.

What do you need to face about your behavior?

—

Facing What We Fear

A play about the courage to be vulnerable and facing our fears

Characters: Paul, the hero is a wrinkled and worn out white haired man of eighty whose sword has turned into a cane. He serves the Maiden.

Maiden is better known as Sara, a princess of auburn hair and twenty summers. She has a lot to learn.

Sara's Dragon, Morgan, is a fiery beast as old as the earth with breath of fire and a soft but jealous spot in his heart for Sara. Yellow Dragon is another dragon that wants to play.

Setting: A summer meadow in a place and time when dragons flourished.

From a hilltop the Hero Paul speaks.

Paul:
I come whenever my maiden Sara calls me. She calls on my swift bloodied sword when her Dragon begins to shake her. Most days, my Maiden rests lovingly on the nose of this mighty beast. During these quiet times, Morgan takes great efforts not to singe her dress or slice her tender cheek with his razor tail. I have learned from many years of careful watch that these two love each other. Funny thing though, every so often my Maiden calls upon me to chop off her beloved's head. I never succeed. Her Dragon shakes my lass when she asks to visit another dragon. Now the Yellow Dragon calls to her.

A Yellow Dragon calls from across the river at the far end of the meadow.

Yellow Dragon:
Come play with me, Maiden.

Paul, the hero, tosses his sword to the ground.

Paul:
All of my Maiden's life she has only known her Dragon. She is also a curious creature. Now I hear her ask her fire-breathing companion something.

Sara:

Please dear Dragon. Let me go across the waters to play with the Yellow Dragon. I will learn new secrets from him that I will share with you.

Fearful of losing his Maiden forever, Morgan the Dragon roars.

Morgan:

No, I will never let you go. No, I can never let you go!

Paul addresses the audience

Paul:

And thus the shaking begins. Fearful, my Maiden calls to me. A million times I have answered her call. Now I fear my sword is no longer sharp. I grow weary through the years. Now my sword feels like a cane. This time I will approach her not with my sword but with new words.

Paul, the weary hero now speaks to Sara as she is caught in the jaws of her fiery companion, Morgan.

Paul:

Maiden I have served you loyally from the moment you were born. Look at me now, my lady. My hair has turned white. My sword has dulled into a cane. I can no longer fight for you. You must talk with your Dragon. Look Morgan in the eye and tell him how you feel. Also listen to him for his feelings are real.

From the Dragon's mouth Sara cries and speaks to her warrior.

Sara:

You leave me now. I am not strong enough to face him alone.

Paul:

Sara, I will not come to your rescue. You must do something. Go to him with your open heart. Face each other.

Morgan has laid Sara on the Earth. The maiden turns to face her Dragon.

Sara:

Morgan, sweet Dragon, you scare me. I don't understand why you shake me so. If I were to play with this Yellow Dragon, I would be gone for the time it takes you to take a deep breath. I can't leave you for long my friend. You

—

are like air to me. I don't think I could live without you. You are the fire in my heart. Know that I love you.

Morgan:
Sara, I can't bear the thought of you leaving me. I fear that you will die far away. Other dragons will tear you to pieces. If you perish, I shall surely follow.

Sara:
Morgan, maybe there is another way. You can come with me. Together, we may play with other dragons and their maidens. Your fiery powers will protect me from the flames of other dragons. And you my Dragon, shall find my words of loving comfort and encouragement bring you love from other maidens. We will take care of each other.

The gentlewoman and fiery beast smile at each other through their tears.

Morgan:
Yes, my Maiden, I will come with you. Take hold of my scaly neck. Together we shall visit the Yellow Dragon and his Maiden.

She climbs on top of his neck, holds on to his ears and they are off.

The wise hero speaks to the audience.

Paul:
I sigh with some relief and some sadness. I, the old warrior must begin to look for a place to rest. Only a moment goes by when I hear a familiar sound that sends a chill through my bones. I turn. Out of the corner of my eye I see the Dragon had returned. My enemy comes close to me. I draw my sword out of fearful habit. To my surprise, he seems to smile.

Morgan reassures his old enemy.

Morgan:
We have not forgotten you. Come rest on me.

Paul:
I look to my Sara, who still rests by his ear. She says it is true. Please rest dear friend. I also climb aboard the scaly back, finding a bed in the fur of the Dragon I close my eyes for the first time and rest.

Exit Sara and Paul as they find comfort on the back of Morgan.

This story reflects a conscious choice I made to change the way I relate to intimate others. I chose to stop fighting love and let it into my life. If I remember to speak my truth as The Maiden did, I do not dissolve. I am also able to rest in the arms of love. Life can be more of a tango than a catfight. Yes.

Assemble the Warriors

I'm not alone.
Spirit is with me.
My ancestors hold my hand.
My friends and family
show up with me,
to dig deep and pay attention.

Who has your back?

How do you show up for yourself?

Sometimes You Can't Be Nice

Sometimes you can't be nice.

Last night during the Presidential debate I was a little snippy, no a lot. I found it bearable to watch by doing the play by play of comments that stood out for me.
Like, "get audited every year" or "somebody give him a tissue" or "It's much less than that…bragadocious?"

I know that I was making fun of a fucked up situation. It is time to continue to love each other, but also to speak out with humanity and courage…

Love.

I am not being passive about this election or my life.

Do something.
Say something.
Write something.
Speak your TRUTH.

What is your truth?

Stop It!!

It's easy to say, "Stop it!"
It's harder to do, I know.
Stop killing each other.
Stop hating each other.

Our nation's underbelly is crusted with fear and hate.
Also love…

Saying "stop" won't really do anything. Two hundred
Congressman on the floor of the House didn't stop it.
Made me proud though, for a moment it made me think:
Maybe, just maybe something more could happen,
like a tough gun law.
It will take millions of us of many colors walking hand in hand,
speaking up,
standing up for each other,
caring for each other.

This moment is history.
Let's make it worth remembering.
Our children are watching,
and worth it.

We are worth it.

Snake Wakes

No judgment.
He wakes. He wants to feed.
You are so nice.
I have a dark side.
Sometimes I'm asleep
and sometimes wide awake.
Temptress.
Powers not understood.
Not yet.
Why?
Now.
Right now.

Top Ten Tips for Moving On

Tip # One

When your grandmother tells you to leave your husband, **just do it**.

Tip # Two

When your grandmother hollers, "**Get out**", question her cautiously.
"You mean grandma, out of your apartment or out of the miserable marriage I find myself in? If at ninety she doesn't roll your suitcase after you, she meant get out of your stinking painful marriage.

Tip # Three

Dedicate several books to your **brilliant grandmother**, even after she passes away.
I am glad I come from you Grandma.

Tip # Four

Come up with a **plan and leave** damn-it!
Don't wait another year hoping he will change.
Take care of yourself. Okay, Grandma.

Tip # Five

I have a plan and I leave my husband, my home, everything I've known for the past five years. **I freak**.

Tip # Six

Freak out safely at a girlfriend's house. She had a spare futon and a large friendly shoulder to cry on. It helps to land where your friend has gone through what you are going through and survived.

Fellow Divorce Survivor
Thank you my Bad Kitty Friend.

Tip # Seven

Beware of the **Tape Monster**. Around this time of boxing stuff up, I learned about the Urban Legend of the Tape Monster. It is said that if you find yourself taping up boxing after 4am, the Tape Monster may find you and get you. When he does you will be found the next day hopefully for your sake breathing all taped up in a box.

I remember this warning and always stop packing after 2am. Please heed my warning.

Tip # Eight

Always return friend's books, pillows, sweaters etc. Keep toothbrushes. I have a nasty habit of borrowing sweaters and not quickly returning them. Sorry my sisters. In a way, maybe your sweater is part of my nesting, making myself feel more comfortable by having something that reminds me of you. "**No, Eve, just give back the sweater**. It was my favorite and I knitted it myself.

Tip # Nine

Stop pity parties and beat up on Eve festivals.
They have been well attended, but too many bruises and heartbreaks. Enough! Just give back the damn sweater.

Tip # Ten

It is okay **to say FUCK you a lot**. Saying "Fuck you, you dirty bastard swine" feels really good.

Boundaries: It's What's For Dinner

Boundaries: It's what's for dinner, lunch, breakfast and 4pm Siesta.

A gal has got to speak up for herself. People sometimes call me weird for speaking up.
I like to say: No, I don't want to. No, you can't make me. No, I am not a doormat. When do I get to the yes?

When you know what you want and you don't want and you speak –
no crying
no screaming.
Speak up.
Speak your truth regardless of what others say.

That is love.
Boundaries are the locks and keys into the heart.
They are forged with wisdom and mistakes.

We all make mistakes.

Welcome to the human race.

Getting Close/F###ing Hard

I don't know how to get close.
I confuse sex with closeness.
I feel close to someone
and I want to have sex.
The wanting to have sex
can result in lots of fear and the possibility of leaving my body.

God damn-it.
This is tough.
I don't know what is real.
The feelings I am feeling right now are uncomfortable and painful.
I realize this is happening
all within me.
I created the situation.
I created the confusion.
I created the pain.
I am fucking myself over right now.

Kindness.
You need some kindness and gentleness.
But you need to be kind to you.
You teach people how to care for and respect you.

I have been here again and again.
I am tired of it.

You will go through it again until you learn.

Learn what?

You are already loved.
You don't have to do anything to be worthy.
You deserve it. You try so hard.
Your heart has been opened up.
You can't hide anymore.
So, please be loving to yourself right now.
I am rooting for you and I believe in you.
No matter what, I have your back,
your front,

however else you need me.

That's good to know. I need you right now.
I feel.
I don't know what I feel.

Stay with this…

I am a sexual being.

Yes, I know.

Something is in my guts and wants to come out.

It is coming out.
Keep writing.

New Doors

"You got the keys to your own life."
-Eve Brownstone

Opening

There is an opening to dive inside.
There is an opening to listen and explore.
There is an opening to ask myself questions and just be
with my own colors and feelings, dancing in the dark.

Inside we roam and battle and sleep.
Inside I learn to trust and stand on both my feet.
I'm on my knees now and looking at my own heart.

You have had a lot going on, Eve.
Rest baby.
The world will continue without you.
You don't have to try so hard.
See you.
Sea you feel the water inside your bones,
inside your blood.
Taste the motion of your waves.

Eve's Tree

Everyday I pass her. Her branches caress the clouds in the sky. She has lived on this land for a thousand years. If there were two of me, we couldn't stretch wide enough to hold her in our arms. She is not meant to be possessed. I do wish to sit under leaves and cool myself from a warm July sun.

I sit under her branches. Her leaves fill my eyes. I wonder what it would be like to travel above the cool darkness and sit in the light on her strong branch. I want to try. I feel I must ask her if I may climb her. I respect her too much to start climbing without her blessing. I also fear her too much. If I do not ask, I may ascend twenty feet in the air on branches that do not wish to hold me and be sent crashing to the earth below. So I shall ask her.

"Dear Tree of a Thousand Years, sitting under your cooling leaves, I have let my eyes wander upwards to where the sun touches you. I have longed to climb to this place of light and feel the sun on my face. May I climb to where the sun may touch both of us?"

The Tree of a Thousand Years speaks to me in the wind.

"You sit under my branches peacefully. You never grab a leaf or charge up my trunk. I feel you are a gentle loving soul. You may climb and know that as you hold on to me I will hold on to you. I will not let you fall."

I listen to my companion. As I rise to my feet, a fear seizes my gut. I have never climbed a tree before, I think to myself. Do I have the strength, the courage and the knowledge?

The Tree senses my fear and says,

"Feel my bark against your feet and begin."

I take off my shoes and socks. I feel her bark under my feet, with my heart beating madly, I begin my climb. On this tree there aren't any low branches. No way to boost myself up. I must find the sturdy crevices and cracks in her bark. I find a crevice two feet off the ground. I put my toes into it. I pull myself up. Also feel my muscles begin to tense. This is a five inch dent, not enough room for all my toes to feel secure. I wrap my arms around her trunk. My mouth is pressed to her bark.

I whisper,

"Please don't let me fall."

I hear a voice in the wind answer me:
"Look for the next crevice."

I search for the next place where I can rest. I see it a foot above me. I lift my body to reach it. I do. This time there is more room to stand. I can rest both feet on this ledge as I look for another place. I am breathing for the moment. I look up to look for another crevice, but all I see is smooth bark for three feet. I grunt and moan.

"Oh, please get me up this tree."

I drag my body up. As I rest again my arm muscles shout to myself
"Was that necessary?"
I answer back,
"No!"

Then I hear the Tree say:

"That was a struggle for you but you did it. Your muscles can support your body. You can. You are enough. See the next place to rest?"

There just above me is the first branch. I climb onto it and sit for a moment. I look up. I see I am I am at least half way there. Above me I can see the rays of sun streaming through the leaves. I feel golden light on my face.

Four feet above me is another branch. I stretch my arm out to grasp it but I can't reach it. I know what I am going to have to do 1. pull myself up the tree up to the next branch. But I notice that I don't groan so much this time. I think to myself, I can climb this tree. Looking down I see how far I have come, fifteen feet.

"Wow!"

I am almost above the leaves. I feel warm inside. I am sweating from the climb. I also feel warmth in some other place in me that has been cold for so long. This warmth is in my fingertips, my legs, in my eyes, even in my hair. My heart is beating not from fear but from this new feeling. I feel the Tree under my fingers. Her bark is firm but she is melting and I am melting. I laugh out loud,

"I love you, Tree."

She speaks clearly now, not from the wind but from herself

"I love you too Eve. You are almost there."

"I know," I say with joy.

Now the climb leads me from branch to branch. Branches are closer together. I need only to stand on one branch to walk on to another. As I continue, the yellow light tenderly covers my body. When I reach the highest branch, I sing.
"I did it! I can climb a very special tree. I can sit in the sun."
The Sun and The Tree of a Thousand Years join together in one voice,

"Yes!"

Up there on the branch in the sun is a place where I do feel good enough. I know that I am somebody. Feeling good enough helps me to be truly myself with others. I stop covering myself up. I am okay. I am not horrible. I can be with other people.   I trust myself more and more.

What gets you out of your comfort zone?

Ancestors

We are what our ancestors prayed for.

We are alive right now to think, speak, act, and be,
for our planet's highest good.

For all beings with beating hearts, blossoms and roots.
There are no mistakes only lessons to learn from, my dear one.

Trust that you will know what to do when the time is right to move,
to speak and to act in Spirit....

Open Eyes

In a lot of my pictures I have my eyes closed.
It is a good metaphor for how I can be
closed off to my feelings.
I feel like I go through periods of healing
where I feel my feelings.
My heart and eyes are open.
Other times not so much.

I admit sometimes I leave my body,
sometimes get quiet,
sometimes isolate,
sometimes fight.
I want people to leave me alone,
but not really.
It is those moments when I really need a hug,
someone to tell me it is ok to feel all of my feelings.
I am safe.

I decide to stay in my body with my eyes open
and feel my feelings.
It's a daily choice.

Ed and Eve

Dearest Eve,

Why do you feel like everybody hates you today? My dear one you are totally projecting your anger on everybody else. Please stop it. People are on your side. You aren't a pain in the ass or draining. You are just being you – a little on the needy side.

Fuck off!

You want to bite people's heads off? Stay with that feeling. You don't have to pretend to be nice. Just be you. Being you is just fine. Just acknowledge the rage you are feeling with that Dragon. The Dragon is your fuel. He keeps you safe.

He keeps people away from me. I feel like I push people away.

You do push people away when you project what you want to disown about yourself. You are not a mean bitch, but part of you is. Part of you would have liked you brother-in-law to have called you back and owned that expectation.

YES

Keep going baby.

I feel like my life is passing me by – like I'm stuck in the basement.

You must get Eve out of the basement.

I want more than just getting out of the basement. I want a one bedroom or studio apartment in a social building by the lake.

I want a friend not to tell people about me living in a basement or having a lack of money when I wasn't getting paid to make me feel less than. I don't need everyone to know things I feel shame about. Not cool. I am writing. Leave me the fuck alone.

Eve, who are you talking to?

—

I'm talking to you, Eddie. No, not you – I want to talk with you. Thanks for coming by.

Stay with me, Eve. Feel. Don't be afraid to show me your inner BITCH.

Fuck off, you mother fucker!

Those are just cuss words. I want to know how your heart really feels.

I don't really know how I feel. There is an edge of anger.
What are you feeling? Stay with the feeling.

I am used to running from my feelings especially if it is a combination of rage and anger.
What am I afraid of?

Stop running away my dear. You are good at that. How would it be to just stay in one place today? You don't have to be any place.

You can be safe to feel. You can be safe to run or do whatever you want.

I prefer you to stay and be with me.

Don't leave the little one inside of you alone with the rage filled one. She is the same!
Spend some time with that young one today. Ask her what she needs.

What do you need precious girl?

<u>Loving</u>

I don't really know what love is. I know love is the only thing that is real.
I have had moments of clarity and warmth fill me and feel me.

It feels like magic – as if God is moving inside of me.
I am so thankful for moments, maybe there is more.
I am thankful for the sun shining on my face and my feet buried in warm
sand.
Sprinklers and laughter tickle me in August.

And the crackle of a fire on a cold January night.
A friend's hand to hold.

I remember the crinkle in your eyes as you smiled at me.
What is real?
That warm sensation I feel now is real. My tears are real.
I don't really understand.
Maybe I am not meant to understand,
just feel it.

Learning

I've learned a thing or two the past sixteen years about coping with change. I've learned you can't solve every problem by moving.

You take yourself with you. It is important to get to know me.

I don't like everything I've found inside of me. I can be a grumpy, bitchy, and needy thing. However, I can also be loving, loyal, smart, and a bit of a badass.

The best feeling has been feeling more and more like I am my own best friend.

"I love you Eve." I tell myself this in the mirror, sometimes without laughing. I am meaning it more and more. You are awesome!!!!

It's okay to be alone. It is a normal part of the human condition. You may fall apart from feeling lonely, but you may come back together as an even better you.

It's important to learn to be ok with having difficult conversations. It's part of being an adult, being real.

You have to tell your boyfriend or lover what you like and don't. He or she can't read your mind. That goes for you identical twins too.

You have to make difficult calls and own up to being human. A "sorry" won't kill you. It will make you stronger.

Before I open my mouth I ask myself, "Is this necessary?
Is this kind and is this right?"
I learned from being married that love is more important than being right.

Receiving

Receiving.

It is second nature for me to give
and share what I have.

It's trickier to receive.
To let stuff in.
I've been known to cry
when people offer
to do nice stuff for me.

Money
Love
Video equipment
Time
Attention

When I open my hands
and receive,
I feel more love
in the depths of me.
I feel more connected
to my loved ones.

Receiving from others makes me feel
like others are walking this road with me.
I so appreciate that.

What are you open to receiving more of?

Heart Opens

Heart opens in winter.

Heart opens in spring.

Heart opens when alone.

Heart opens with friends.

Heart opens in the Sun
and in the rain.

Heart opens…breathe.

Heart opens.
Keep your eyes open too.

Stay.
Stay open.

Falling

It seems I have spent my life falling in love. More like falling on my face. I don't think I was ever in love with the real person, just an illusion of who I thought I saw or how I wanted them to be.

I find myself attracted to the strong and complicated types.
People who feel too much or nothing at all. Or the really angry…growling and controlling…that's also me though, if I don't own my own anger …for that matter all my feelings. I am up shits creek…for realz.

In relationships, I put on my tool belt and attempt to tweak boyfriends here or there. Doesn't work! Step the fuck off!! I can't change or fix anyone. I can only change myself.

A friend reminded me at Jarvis Beach:
"If you fall, land on your feet…if you can't land on your feet, laugh before you land on your face."
Thanks Kathy.

Lately, I have been way too serious about the choices I've made. I'm taking a lot of anger out on myself.

"Fuck you, Eve. You are a monster and nobody loves you!!!"-Brutal self-talk.

This morning at the end of Jarvis pier, I was looking for a sign and message from my higher power. It came in the form of a wave that washed over me. I laughed out loud. Thank you God for helping me not to take myself so seriously.

Love,
Eve

Surrender in the Waves

I let the wind carry me down to Pratt Beach.
The full moon guides my footsteps.
I look for you in the water.
I hope to see your smile and touch your skin.
Are you real?
Are you a lake spirit come to calm my body and move my soul?

Stir my liquid with your mouth.

I thought of you the night before, waiting for me on the pier.
Thoughts of your hand on my back and slipping my shirt over my head
made me want to stay by the water to imagine us swimming together,
wrestling in the waves.

I pull you close to me.

I feel your firm lips everywhere
and your strong legs surround me and lift me up.
I taste your neck, your broad shoulders.
I feel myself float as I rest in your arms
I want this surrender.

Hello

I can't see you. I feel you.

I feel your breath on my neck and your heat through my belly.

Step closer and I can hear you call my name.
Sometimes I see you out at the end of the pier.

There is sunlight on your cheek.
Your eyes are glowing with a few tears.

It's ok.
It's nice to see you.

Happy

This morning I slept in and got up with a smile on my face. I was surprised. Yom Kippur is usually a reflective and sometimes sad time for me. But something shifted in me over time. Even if this feeling is just for today, I want to mark it. I want to honor this feeling I have.

Happiness.

It stems from a dream I had early this morning. This young woman that I was at 21 was smiling in this dream. She had been through so much before this picture was taken. She had survived a year in Israel and rape. In my dream she was sitting with friends and just laughing and smiling. She looked at me and smiled. Even after all she had been through. She was letting me know that she was ok. She was letting me know that she was more than ok and that I was more than ok. I could laugh and feel happy too.

Thank you my dear girl at 21. Thank you for the gift of reminding me who I really am.

Being with Myself

Wherever I go I take myself with me --
To the beach,
To Bordeaux France, or a friend's couch.

I am house sitting for friends who are in Ecuador this week.
Being by myself is hardest at night.
I'd like to cuddle with someone.

Mornings at sunrise are easier
because I feel held by the lake and the sun.
They are good friends.

Key To My Own Life

I always tell my clients (usually women) to "Get your keys back."

How do you get your damn key back? First of all realize that you have given your key
or power away to your own damn life.

Then do what feeds your soul. Read a good book, paint, run a marathon.
Take yourself on a trip overseas, cuddle with your dog, or do the Conga with friends.
Do you.
Feed your soul. Love yourself.
Make your own damn key.

You got this!

What are the keys to your life?

Women's Empowerment

What does woman's power look like?

Connection
Compassion
Relational

Men are also beginning to understand and embrace this kind of power.
We saw this in Obama.

We hold each other up.
We are in this together.
We are part of a tribe
where everyone is fed
and everyone drinks
when thirsty.

There is enough to go around.

Home

What makes a home?

What makes a home? Is it the brick, cement, metal and wood that create a home? It is what the heart knows, connections between loved ones, the feeling of being held with love and safety. It is the feeling of being seen as good enough and encouraged to go for what you want, even if it involves leaving home to make your dreams come true.

As you make your journey into to this unknown adventure, you find that your home is still with you in your heart. It says to you, "We are with you, you are safe and you can do this." Your sense of home is reflected in the way you say "hello", help out a friend, and stand up for yourself. Home is also a place you may return to again and again. You are welcomed with open arms.

Love Is What You Feel

I'm trying to pin love down.
I'm trying to understand love.

Paint a pretty picture.

I want to put love in a box
that I can carry around,
but it's not happening.

That isn't how love works.

Can you tell me how love works?

        No, Eve …you just gotta feel it.

I Got This!

I got this.

Thirty years ago I freaked out about being separated from my twin. She decided to go to a different college in another state. It was rough when I was eighteen. I wasn't sure if I could make it. I literally wasn't sure if I could survive without her. My twin and I took care of each other growing up – ever since conception.

After thirty years it sunk in that I got this:
I got this living on my own and showing up for myself thing.
You have to be tough to live on your own.

In relationship time and again I have wanted to be taken care of and look to someone else to help me make decisions. That's what I am used to. But my relationships have led to heartache. I have learned that I don't have to keep doing the same thing.

I remember that my name is Eve. My soul and spirit have been here many times before.
I do know a few things. I know that the most important key to my life is Self-Love and I am getting there. I am working, playing, and being in my life one day at a time.

About Author

Eve is the author of *Opening New Doors*, a book of poetry and process, which examines a journey from fear to love. *Letting Go/Going On*, is a booklet for healing from trauma. *Born In Relationship* tells the story of one identical twin's search for herself and healthy relationships. Her work has been featured in the Boston Globe, Chicago Tribune and The WGN Morning Show.

Eve lives and works as an expressive arts therapist in Chicago.. Most mornings you can find Eve down at the beach to meet the sunrise. The photos included here are just a few taken from 2012-2017.

You can reach Eve at brownstonetherapeutics@gmail.com.

Acknowledgements

This book is twenty-six years in the making. This journey started back at Lesley College in graduate school, where I learned that I was more than just one of "The Twins". I was Eve.

Thanks to Margot, Paulo, Shaun, Peter and Elaine for seeing me.

Big thanks to my editor Eric Allen Yankee for his skills and handholding.

Thanks to my buddies at the Royal Soul's Open Mic who created a safe space for me and many others to share our writing.

Thanks to my parents Peter and Judy for loving me as best they could.

Thanks to my sisters Laura and Caty for being themselves and Malcolm and Delaine for believing that I could write.

Thanks to my friends who show up for me and let me know I'm welcome when I show up for them.

Thanks to Charmers Café for being my place for coffee and writing.

Thanks to you readers for stopping for a while to read.
You got this!

NOTES 1

NOTES 2

NOTES 3

I GOT THIS!

by

Eve Brownstone

43104133R00045

Made in the USA
Middletown, DE
30 April 2017